Sing-along Songs

This book belongs to:

....

The Wheels on the Bus

The wheels on the bus go round and round,

Round and round,

Round and round.

The wheels on the bus go round and round,

All through the town.

Round and round!

The horn on the bus goes "Beep, beep, beep,
Beep, beep, beep,
Beep, beep, beep".
The horn on the bus goes "Beep, beep, beep",
All through the town.

Beep, beep, beep!

Turn
the
page!

The wipers on the bus go "Swish, swish, swish,
Swish, swish, swish,
Swish, swish, swish".
The wipers on the bus go "Swish, swish, swish",
All through the town.

The driver on the bus says "Move on back,
Move on back,
Move on back".
The driver on the bus says "Move on back",
All through the town.

The babies on the bus go "Waa, waa, waa,

Waa, waa, waa,

Waa, waa, waa".

The babies on the bus go "Waa, waa, waa",

All through the town.

The people on the bus go "Shh, shh, shh,

Shh, shh, shh,

Shh, shh, shh".

The people on the bus go "Shh, shh, shh",

All through the town.

This Old Man

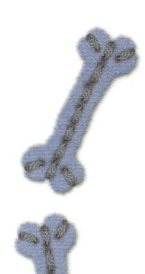

This old man, he played one,

He played knick-knack on my drum;

With a knick-knack paddy whack, give a dog a bone,

This old man came rolling home.

This old man, he played two,

He played knick-knack on my shoe;

With a knick-knack paddy whack, give a dog a bone,

This old man came rolling home.

This old man, he played three,

He played knick-knack on my knee;

With a knick-knack paddy whack, give a dog a bone,

This old man came rolling home.

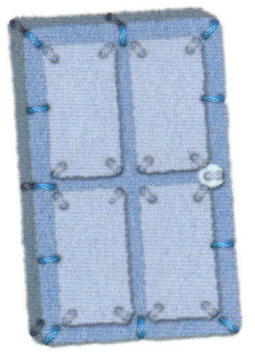

This old man, he played four,
He played knick-knack on my door;
With a knick-knack paddy whack, give a dog a bone,
This old man came rolling home.

This old man, he played five,
He played knick-knack on my hive;
With a knick-knack paddy whack, give a dog a bone,
This old man came rolling home.

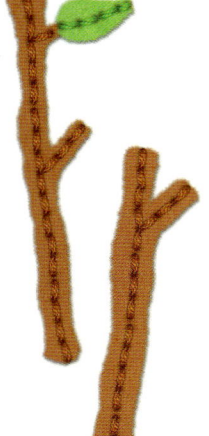

This old man, he played six,
He played knick-knack on my sticks;
With a knick-knack paddy whack, give a dog a bone,
This old man came rolling home.

Turn the page!

This old man, he played seven,
He played knick-knack up in Heaven;
With a knick-knack paddy whack, give a dog a bone,
This old man came rolling home.

This old man, he played eight,
He played knick-knack on my gate;
With a knick-knack paddy whack, give a dog a bone,
This old man came rolling home.

This old man, he played nine,
He played knick-knack on my spine;
With a knick-knack paddy whack, give a dog a bone,
This old man came rolling home.

This old man, he played ten,
He played knick-knack once again;
With a knick-knack paddy whack, give a dog a bone,
This old man came rolling home.

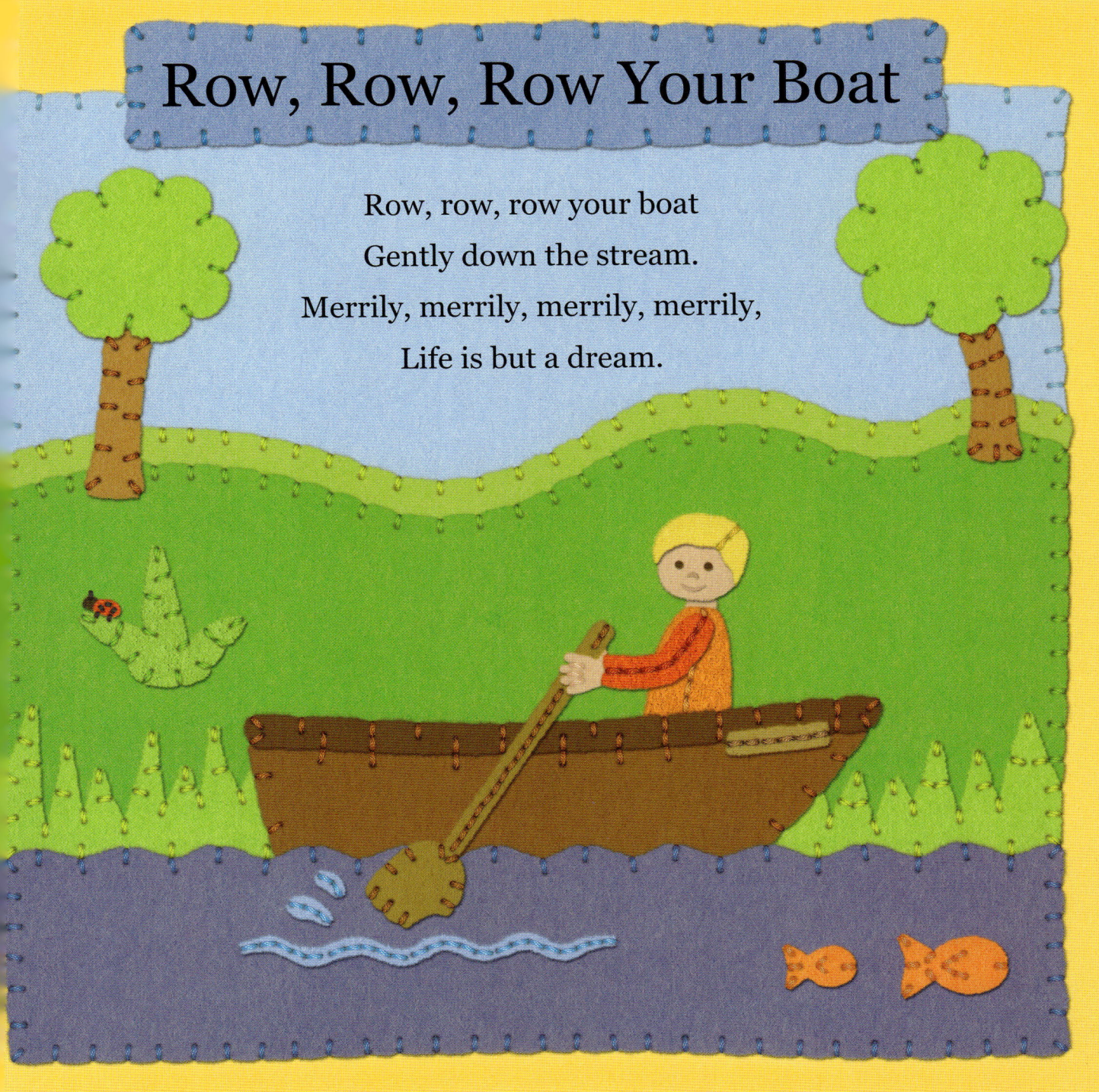

Row, Row, Row Your Boat

Row, row, row your boat
Gently down the stream.
Merrily, merrily, merrily, merrily,
Life is but a dream.

Old Macdonald

Old Macdonald had a farm, E I E I O!

And on his farm he had a cow, E I E I O!

With a "moo moo" here and a "moo moo" there,

Here a "moo", there a "moo"

Everywhere a "moo moo",

Old Macdonald had a farm, E I E I O!

Old Macdonald had a farm, E I E I O!

And on his farm he had a pig, E I E I O!

With an "oink oink" here and an "oink oink" there,

Here an "oink", there an "oink"

Everywhere an "oink oink",

"Moo moo" here and a "moo moo" there,

Here a "moo", there a "moo"

Everywhere a "moo moo",

Old Macdonald had a farm, E I E I O!

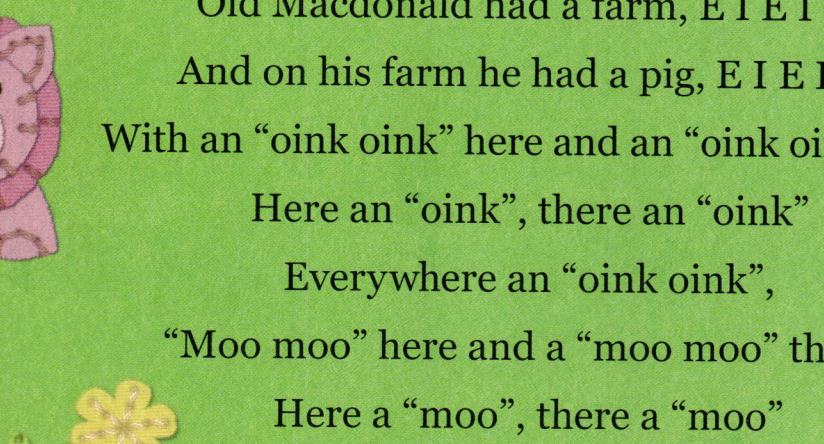
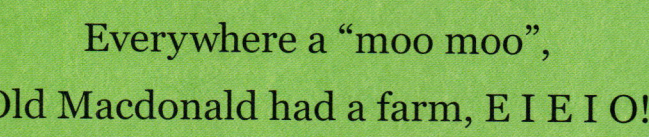

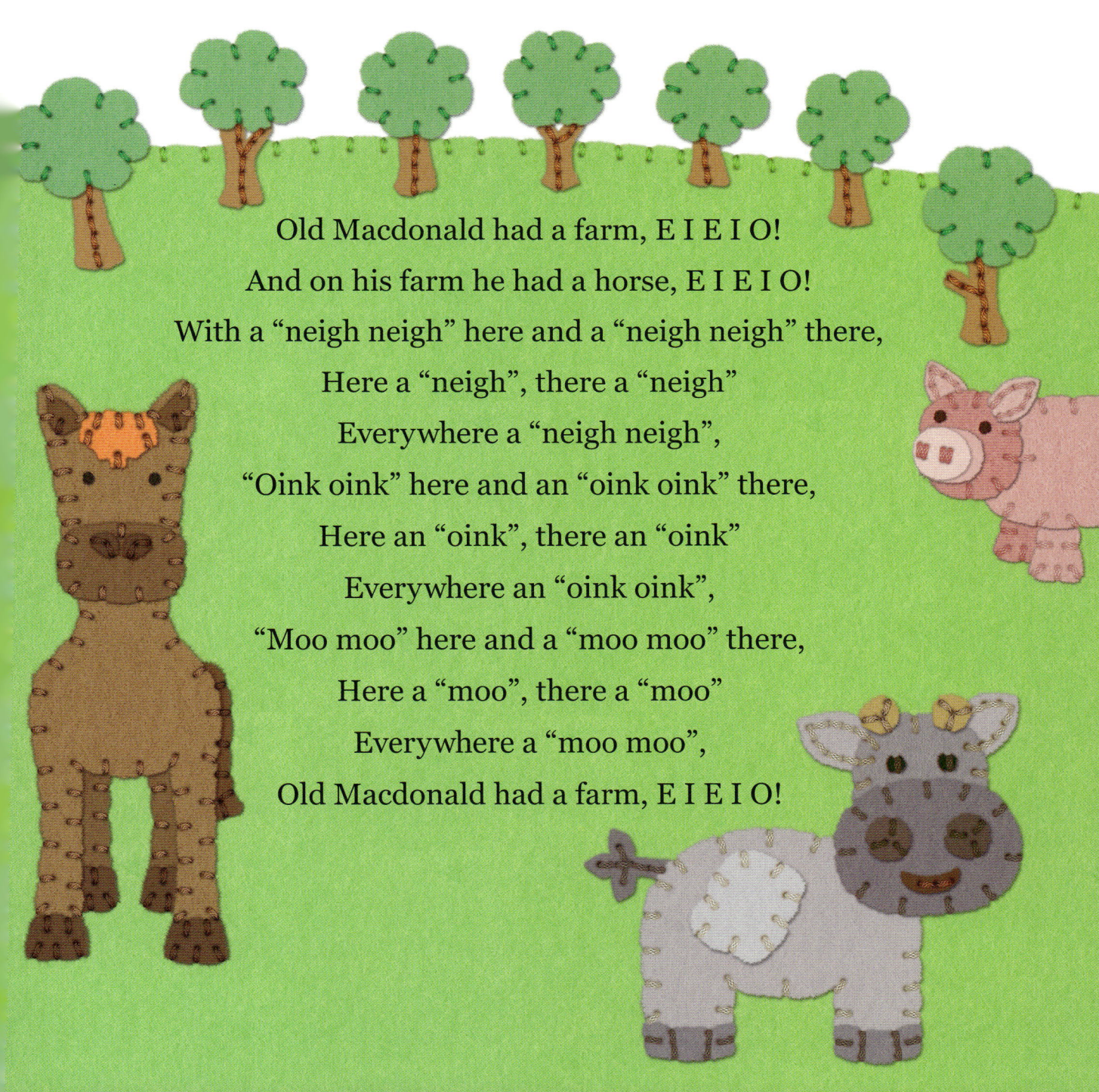

Old Macdonald had a farm, E I E I O!
And on his farm he had a horse, E I E I O!
With a "neigh neigh" here and a "neigh neigh" there,
Here a "neigh", there a "neigh"
Everywhere a "neigh neigh",
"Oink oink" here and an "oink oink" there,
Here an "oink", there an "oink"
Everywhere an "oink oink",
"Moo moo" here and a "moo moo" there,
Here a "moo", there a "moo"
Everywhere a "moo moo",
Old Macdonald had a farm, E I E I O!

She'll Be Coming Round the Mountain

She'll be coming round the mountain when she comes
She'll be coming round the mountain when she comes
She'll be coming round the mountain,
She'll be coming round the mountain,
She'll be coming round the mountain when she comes.

She'll be driving six white horses when she comes
She'll be driving six white horses when she comes
She'll be driving six white horses,
She'll be driving six white horses,
She'll be driving six white horses when she comes.

Oh we'll all go out to meet her when she comes
Oh we'll all go out to meet her when she comes
Oh we'll all go out to meet her,
Oh we'll all go out to meet her,
Oh we'll all go out to meet her when she comes.

She'll be wearing red pajamas when she comes

She'll be wearing red pajamas when she comes

She'll be wearing red pajamas,

She'll be wearing red pajamas,

She'll be wearing red pajamas when she comes.

She will have to sleep with grandma when she comes

She will have to sleep with grandma when she comes

She will have to sleep with grandma,

She will have to sleep with grandma,

She will have to sleep with grandma when she comes.

If You're Happy and You Know It

If you're happy and you know it, clap your hands!

If you're happy and you know it, clap your hands!

If you're happy and you know it,

Then your face will surely show it,

If you're happy and you know it, clap your hands!

If you're happy and you know it, stomp your feet!

If you're happy and you know it, stomp your feet!

If you're happy and you know it,

Then your face will surely show it,

If you're happy and you know it, stomp your feet!

If you're happy and you know it, shout hooray!
If you're happy and you know it, shout hooray!
If you're happy and you know it,
Then your face will surely show it,
If you're happy and you know it, shout hooray!

If you're happy and you know it, do all three!
If you're happy and you know it, do all three!
If you're happy and you know it,
Then your face will surely show it,
If you're happy and you know it, do all three!

Do Your Ears Hang Low?

Do your ears hang low?
Do they wobble to and fro?
Can you tie them in a knot?
Can you tie them in a bow?
Can you throw them o'er your shoulder
Like a continental soldier?
Do your ears hang low?

Do your ears hang high?
Do they reach up to the sky?
Do they droop when they are wet?
Do they stiffen when they're dry?
Can you semaphore your neighbor
With a minimum of labor?
Do your ears hang high?

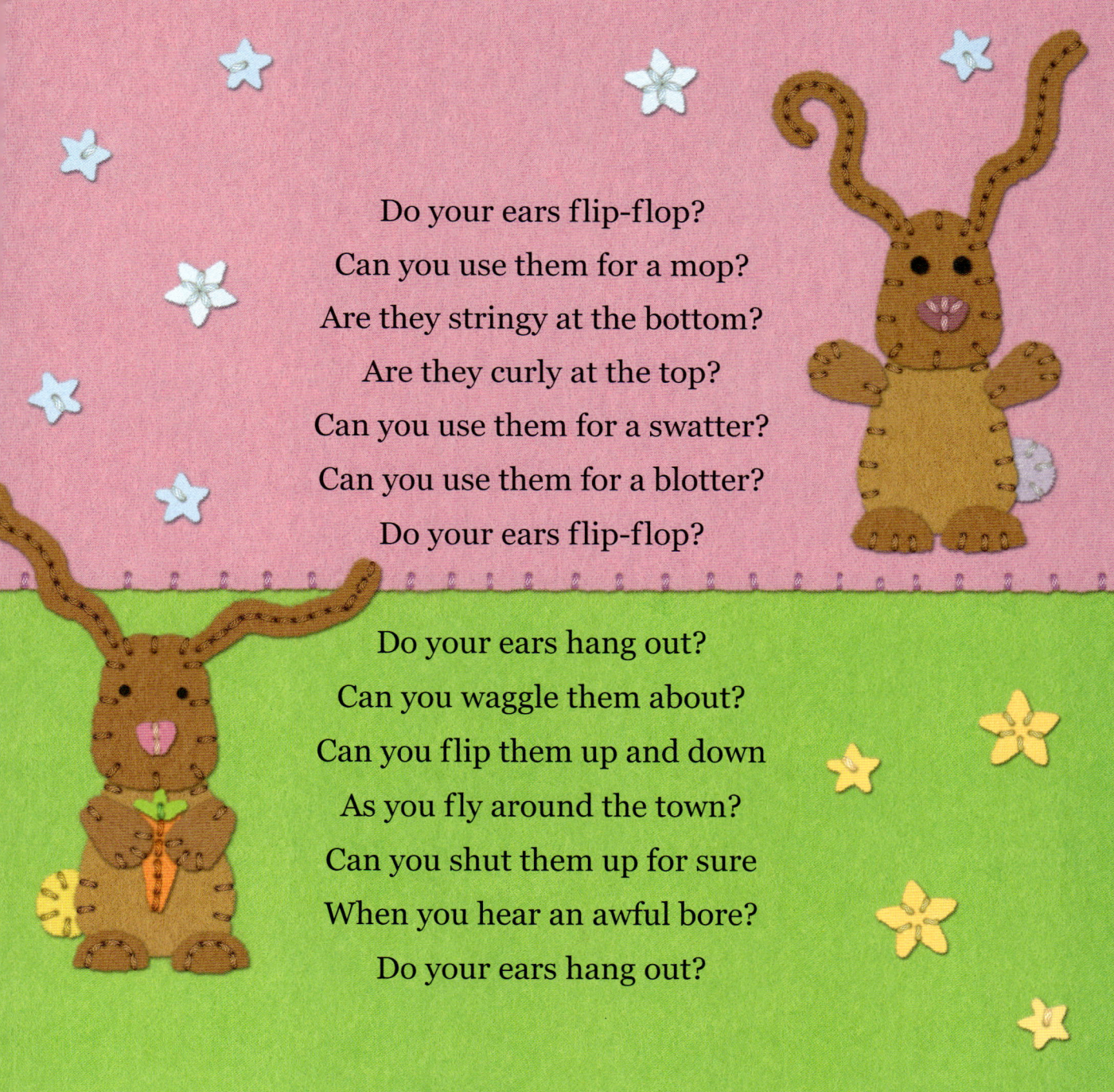

Do your ears flip-flop?

Can you use them for a mop?

Are they stringy at the bottom?

Are they curly at the top?

Can you use them for a swatter?

Can you use them for a blotter?

Do your ears flip-flop?

Do your ears hang out?

Can you waggle them about?

Can you flip them up and down

As you fly around the town?

Can you shut them up for sure

When you hear an awful bore?

Do your ears hang out?

London Bridge

London Bridge is falling down,
Falling down, falling down.
London Bridge is falling down,
My fair lady!

Build it up with iron bars,
Iron bars, iron bars.
Build it up with iron bars,
My fair lady!

Iron bars will bend and break,
Bend and break, bend and break.
Iron bars will bend and break,
My fair lady!

Here's a prisoner I have caught,
I have caught, I have caught.
Here's a prisoner I have caught,
My fair lady!

Off to prison he must go,
He must go, he must go.
Off to prison he must go,
My fair lady!

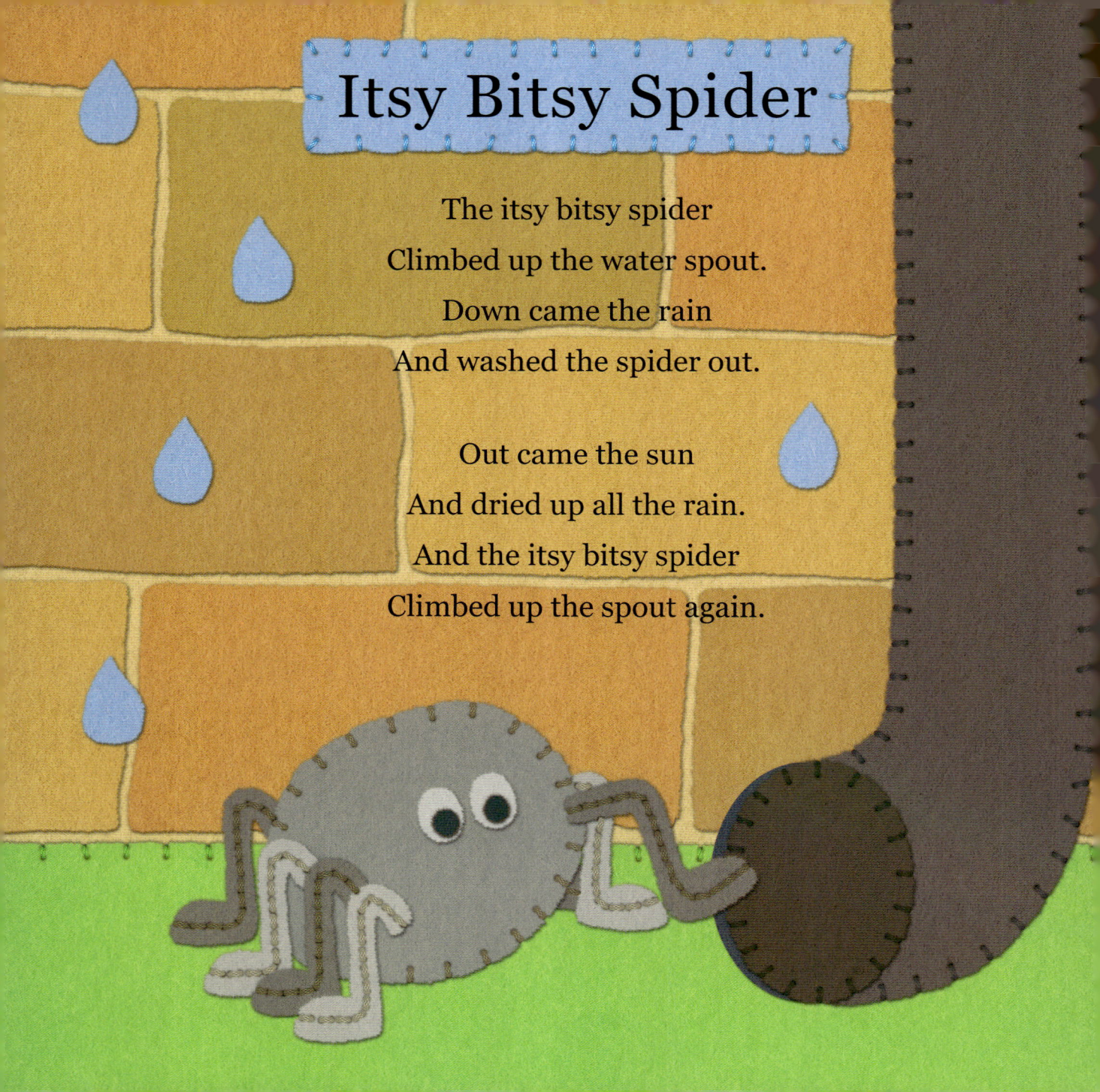

Itsy Bitsy Spider

The itsy bitsy spider
Climbed up the water spout.
Down came the rain
And washed the spider out.

Out came the sun
And dried up all the rain.
And the itsy bitsy spider
Climbed up the spout again.

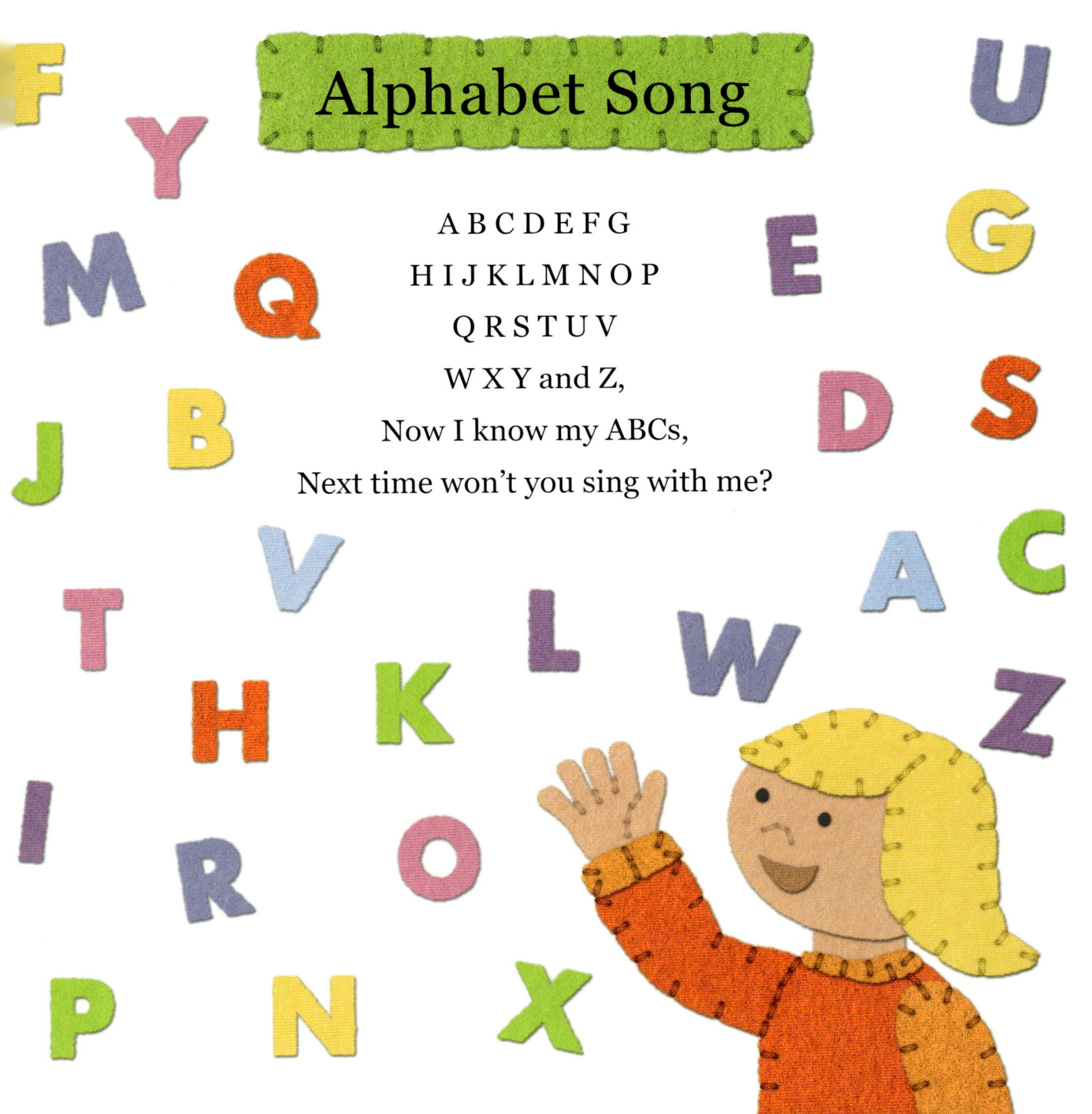

Alphabet Song

A B C D E F G
H I J K L M N O P
Q R S T U V
W X Y and Z,
Now I know my ABCs,
Next time won't you sing with me?

Bingo

There was a farmer had a dog
And Bingo was his name-o.
B I N G O!
B I N G O!
B I N G O!
And Bingo was his name-o!

There was a farmer had a dog
And Bingo was his name-o.
(Clap) I N G O!
(Clap) I N G O!
(Clap) I N G O!
And Bingo was his name-o!

There was a farmer had a dog
And Bingo was his name-o.
(Clap) (clap) N G O!
(Clap) (clap) N G O!
(Clap) (clap) N G O!
And Bingo was his name-o!

There was a farmer had a dog
And Bingo was his name-o.
(Clap) (clap) (clap) G O!
(Clap) (clap) (clap) G O!
(Clap) (clap) (clap) G O!
And Bingo was his name-o!

Turn the page!

There was a farmer had a dog
And Bingo was his name-o.
(Clap) (clap) (clap) (clap) O!
(Clap) (clap) (clap) (clap) O!
(Clap) (clap) (clap) (clap) O!
And Bingo was his name-o!

There was a farmer had a dog
And Bingo was his name-o.
(Clap) (clap) (clap) (clap) (clap)
(Clap) (clap) (clap) (clap) (clap)
(Clap) (clap) (clap) (clap) (clap)
And Bingo was his name-o!

The More We Get Together

The more we get together,

Together, together,

The more we get together,

The happier we'll be.

For your friends are my friends,

And my friends are your friends,

The more we get together,

The happier we'll be!

I Had a Little Nut Tree

I had a little nut tree,
Nothing would it bear,
But a silver nutmeg
And a golden pear.

The King of Spain's daughter
Came to visit me,
And all for the sake
Of my little nut tree.

I skipped over the ocean,
I danced over the sea,
And all the birds in the air
Couldn't catch me.